Copyright © 2020 Sanaii Fourcand

All rights reserved. No part of this publication may be reproduced, distributed, or transmitted in any form or by any means, including photocopying, recording, or other electronic or mechanical methods, without the prior written permission of the publisher, except in the case of brief quotations embodied in reviews and certain other non-commercial uses permitted by copyright law.

Any internet addresses, phone numbers, or company or product information printed in this book are offered as a resource and are not intended in any way to be or to imply an endorsement by the publisher, nor does the publisher vouch for the existence, content, or services of these sites, phone numbers, companies, or products beyond the life of this book

ISBN 978-1-7342191-2-8

Published by Believe In Your Book Publishing

Printed in the United States of America

For permission request, write to the publisher, addressed
"Attention: Permissions Coordinator/ to the address below.

Email: BiybPublishing@gmail.com

I believe in me

This Beautiful Journal Belongs To:

_____

Hey you, yeah you,
I know that you will enjoy this journal and all of the wonderful things kept inside. I know that sometimes school can be tough, friends can be mean, and things don't always go your way. But, I just wanted you to know, no matter what you are going through, or what people say about you, you are beautiful. You are an amazing person, that has so many dreams inside of you just waiting to unleash into greatness. So, don't ever be afraid to stand out, because you were born to be different. I just want you to know that I love you and God loves you.

Love,

Sanaii Sky

Feel Free to answer the questions with:
words, stickers, images and/or drawing! Have fun and enjoy your Journal!

Don't forget to smile :)

What makes you unique?

What do you like most about yourself?

What are you most proud of?

What are your goals for this school year?

What are some dreams you want to accomplish?

What are some things you want?

Explain, your fashion style?

What makes you slay all day?

What do you want to be when you grow up?

What college do you want to go to?

Who inspires you?

What is your favorite color(s)?

What is your favorite hair style?

What is your friends name?

I believe in me

I Believe in Me

Affirmations are speaking positive things over your life daily. Words are powerful, so remember to speak only nice things about yourself.

Repeat Daily

I AM Beautiful
I AM Healthy
I AM Wealthy
I AM a Young Woman of God
I AM a straight **'A'** student
I AM going to have an Amazing Day
I AM Successful
I AM Educated
I AM Confident
I Believe in Me
I Believe in Myself
I AM Loving
I AM a Great role model
I AM a Giver
I AM Rich
I AM Wavy All of the Time
I AM Proud to be Me
I Slay All Day
God Loves Me
I AM a Leader
I AM Blessed

Vision Board

Take a moment and create a Vision Board! Add pictures, stickers, words & fun things you will like to have this year. Enjoy!

Vision Board

Take a moment and create a Vision Board! Add pictures, stickers, words & fun things you will like to have this year. Enjoy!

**Feel free to express how your day was today. You can use stickers, drawing and/or words.
Be creative and have fun!**

Daily Check:

Use a sticker to describe your day	How was your day?	What did you do?	What did you like the most?

Daily Check:

	Use a sticker to describe your day	How was your day?	What did you do?	What did you like the most?
MONDAY				
TUESDAY				
WEDNESDAY				
THURSDSAY				
FRIDAY				
SATURDAY				
SUNDAY				

Daily Check:

Use a sticker to describe your day	How was your day?	What did you do?	What did you like the most?

Daily Check:

	Use a sticker to describe your day	How was your day?	What did you do?	What did you like the most?
MONDAY				
TUESDAY				
WEDNESDAY				
THURSDSAY				
FRIDAY				
SATURDAY				
SUNDAY				

Now that you have completed all the fun activities:
From this point forward, write down your thoughts, feeling and goals for the future.
Enjoy!

I Believe in Me

I Believe in Me

I Believe in Me

I Believe in Me

I Believe in Me

I Believe in Me

I Believe in Me

I Believe in Me

I Believe in Me

I Believe in Me

I Believe in Me

I Believe in Me

I Believe in Me

I Believe in Me

I Believe in Me

I Believe in Me

I Believe in Me

I Believe in Me

I Believe in Me

I Believe in Me

I Believe in Me

I Believe in Me

I Believe in Me

I Believe in Me

I Believe in Me

I Believe in Me

I Believe in Me

I Believe in Me

I Believe in Me

I Believe in Me

I Believe in Me

I Believe in Me

I Believe in Me

I Believe in Me

I Believe in Me

I Believe in Me

I Believe in Me

I Believe in Me

I Believe in Me

I Believe in Me

I Believe in Me

I Believe in Me

I Believe in Me

www.ingramcontent.com/pod-product-compliance
Lightning Source LLC
Chambersburg PA
CBHW042129100526
44587CB00026B/4221